BEANO
BO
2011
2011
M

THE BASH STREET KIDS

SORT OUT THAT CLASS OF YOURS! AND SMARTEN UP, YOU SCRUFF!
SIGH, THERE'S POSH STREET'S TEACHER WITH ALL HIS TEACHING PRIZES.
HYUK HYUK.

IN SCHOOL...
BOOT
PONK
HELLO...
TOSS

...OH, WHY DO I BOTHER?
YEOW!
TUG
WHAT'S UP WITH TEACHER?
THUD
CRACK
DUNNO, MATE. LET'S ASK HIM.

WHAT'S UP, TEACHER?
OH, NOTHING MUCH REALLY...

COME ON... YOU CAN TELL US.
YEAH, WE'LL READ YOUR MAIL AND FIND OUT LATER ANYWAY.
NUDGE
NUDGE

IT'S THE TEACHER OF THE YEAR AWARDS TONIGHT AND THE BIG PRIZE, THE GOLDEN MORTARBOARDS, ARE BEING HANDED OUT.
TEACHER OF THE YEAR AWARDS TONIGHT.

I NEVER GET NOMINATED FOR AN AWARD - I NEVER EVEN GET INVITED TO CLAP FOR THE OTHER TEACHERS.
WHY NOT?

LOOK AT YOU UNTEACHABLE LOT.
EEK!
GRRR!
GRRR!
BZZZZ
OOF!
THUD!
ZOOM!

RIGHT, FORGET I ASKED THAT, OKAY?
PAT
SPIT
BITE

OH, NEVER MIND. IT DOESN'T MATTER...
POOR OLD TEACHER. TIME FOR A SECRET MEETING, PEOPLE.

SO...
THIS MEETING IS CALLED TO ORDER.
Meeting in Progress

WE HAVE GOT TO GET A BIGGER MEETING PLACE.

FORGET THAT. WE'RE GOING TO HELP TEACHER GET NOMINATED FOR A TEACHER OF THE YEAR AWARD. WE NEED TO SMARTEN UP.
CAN'T WE JUST GO TO MARS? IT WOULD BE A LOT EASIER.

THE SMARTENING UP BEGINS...
YEOW! MY HAIR GOT BRUSHED LAST YEAR, TOOTS!
QUIT HOWLING. DANNY SAID WE NEED TO SMARTEN UP AND THAT INCLUDES YOU, SIDNEY!
TUG

YOU'LL NEVER FIT INTO YOUR UNIFORM, PLUG. YOU'VE GROWN A BIT SINCE YOU GOT IT.
PING
PING
WELL, JUST A BIT - BUT I WAS STILL A HANDSOME LAD BACK THEN.
CAFE
NEARBY...
WHERE'S MY STREET SWEEPER BUGGY GONE?
MEE-YEAAOOWW! PERFECT FOR THE SCHOOL YARD.
STREET SWEEPER
VROOM
SWEEP

IN CLASS...
WE'LL START WITH SOMETHING SIMPLE. 2 PLUS 2 IS...?
2 + 2 =

2+2=
I KNOW I SAID WE'D START WITH SOMETHING SIMPLE BUT I DIDN'T THINK IT WOULD BE SMIFFY. I'M ALMOST AFRAID TO ASK, BUT ON YOU GO, SMIFFY. DO YOU KNOW?

FOUR!
EH? I MEAN, ER, YES, CORRECT.
WIPE!
WELL DONE, SMIFFY.
GOOD WORK US! THROWING MY VOICE AND WORKING SMIFFY LIKE A PUPPET.
HOW TO THROW YOUR VOICE
WHAT'S A SMIFFY?
THAT WAS WELL DONE, CLASS, BUT HERE'S A TOUGHER QUESTION. WHAT'S THE CAPITAL OF INDONESIA?
I'M SUNK. THEY'LL NEVER GET IT.
SMUG

INDONESIA'S CAPITAL? JAKARTA!
ER, LET ME CHECK. YES, YES, THAT'S RIGHT, DANNY.
HOW DID HE KNOW THAT?

THE SCHOOL SECURITY OFFICE...
NNNGGHHH!
II B SECURITY CAMERA
WHEN WAS THE GREAT FIRE OF LONDON?
I CAN SEE THE NEXT QUESTION.
SEARCH
I'LL GET THE ANSWER OFF THE INTERNET.

THE INTERWEB IS GREAT!
WHEN WAS THE GREAT FIRE OF LONDON?
TAP-TAP
CAN YOU HEAR ME ON YOUR HEADPHONES, DANNY? THE ANSWER IS... 1666!
YIKES! LOUD!
HOW TO THROW YOUR VOICE
I THOUGHT I WAS QUITE QUIETLY SPOKEN.
THE GREAT FIRE OF LONDON WAS IN 1666.
WRO... OH, WAIT. THAT'S RIGHT, TOO. WELL DONE.
IT'S AMAZING. THEY GOT ALL THE QUESTIONS RIGHT.
THIS IS A SPLENDID CLASS. I'M GOING TO NOMINATE YOU FOR AN AWARD, TEACHER. YOU MUST COME TO THE TEACHER OF THE YEAR AWARDS TONIGHT.
NOM... NOM...
PUNCH
PUNCH
...NOMINATED!
CLICK!
THINK HE'S HAPPY ABOUT IT, MATE?
WHO'S HAPPY ABOUT WHAT?

BASH ST. SCHOOL
HELLO? MRS TEACHER? GET YOUR BEST DRESS. WE'RE GOING TO THE AWARDS!
JUST A BIT, MATE.
SKIP.
THAT NIGHT..
TEACHER OF THE YEAR AWARDS
HM...
CLICK
CLICK
I ALWAYS WANTED TO COME HERE.
THERE'S FIT FLANAGAN - HE'S BEEN P.E. TEACHER OF THE YEAR 7 YEARS RUNNING - AND 4 YEARS JOGGING. BEHIND HIM THAT'S DETENTION DAVIES. HE'S GIVEN MORE DETENTION THAN ANY OTHER TEACHER EVER. HE'S MY HERO.
HIYA, TEACHER!
WHAT ARE YOU LOT DOING HERE?
THIS IS A POSH EVENING FOR US TEACHERS - WE'VE WORKED HARD FOR IT! GO AWAY!
AFTER ALL WE DID FOR YOU?
AW.
LET'S MEET THE MAYOR, DEAREST.
WHAT AN UNGRATEFUL OLD BOGEY!
WELL, IF HE WANTS TO MEET THE MAYOR...

ON THE COUNT OF THREE, FLIP THE CARPET. 1...2...
CONCENTRATING ON HIS NUMBERS
FLIP!
PYOING
WHAT COMES AFTER 2?
...3!
TUG
TUG
EEKS!
RIPPLING WAVE
CLICK
THUD
TEACHER! I KNEW I SHOULDN'T HAVE INVITED HIM!
I WONDER IF TEACHER HAS SEEN THIS?
DAILY BLAH
UNRULY TEACHER KICKED OUT OF AWARDS
SOB SOB WEEP WAIL
I'D SAY HE PROBABLY HAS.
DON'T FEEL BAD, TEACHER.
PAT! PAT!
SOON...
THIS IS FROM US FOR YOU.
YEAH.
A GOLDEN MORTARBOARD?
for Sir

I ALWAYS WANTED ONE! THIS IS THE BEST THING THAT'S EVER HAPPENED TO ME!
SNATCH
HUG
for sir
NOW, HAS ANYONE SEEN MY USUAL MORTARBOARD?
YOU'RE GOING TO TELL ME THIS IS MY OWN MORTARBOARD, AREN'T YOU?
YEP.
NOD
NOD
AND I'M COVERED IN GOLD PAINT NOW, AMN'T I?
WELL... YEAH.
YOU KNOW SOMETHING? THAT'S STILL THE NICEST THING THEY'VE EVER DONE FOR ME! THEY'RE NOT SO BAD REALLY.
WATER BOMB
PUFF
BLOW
CHUFF
BOOT
HOOF
DS

FRED'S BED

FREDS BED 010A

FREDS BED 0108

HMM. MY BED SEEMS TO HAVE SHRUNK.

5 MINUTES PREVIOUSLY... YOU KNOW THE REST! -
RIGHT, FRED. YOU CAN HAVE A PIECE OF THE CAKE NOW THAT YOU'VE EATEN YOUR TEA.
BLOIK. DON'T KNOW IF I CAN MANAGE, BUT I'LL SOLDIER ON.

YOU KNOW SOMETHING... I'M FEELING A LITTLE...

..SICK...GROOO...
SPLURK!

HOW ON EARTH COULD ONE TINY BITE OF CAKE MAKE YOU SO ILL, FRED?

THEY ALWAYS SAY THAT "MOTHER KNOWS BEST" AND I C'N SEE WHY NOW.

MINNIE
The
MINX
IF I WAS AN ANIMAL, WHAT KIND OF ANIMAL WOULD I BE?

LET'S FIND OUT.

I'M AN ELLYFANT.
HOOVOR

SCOFF! GOBBLE! MUNCH!
PARP!
THERE'S MY OLD MATE, FATTY FUDGE, SCOFFING BUNS, TOO.

SOOOK!
SHE'S PINCHED MY BUNS!
AND US ELLYFANTS JUST LOVE BUNS. I'LL HAVE THOSE.

OI! SHE'S HAD THE LOT!
THANKS FOR FEEDING THE WILDLIFE, FATTY.

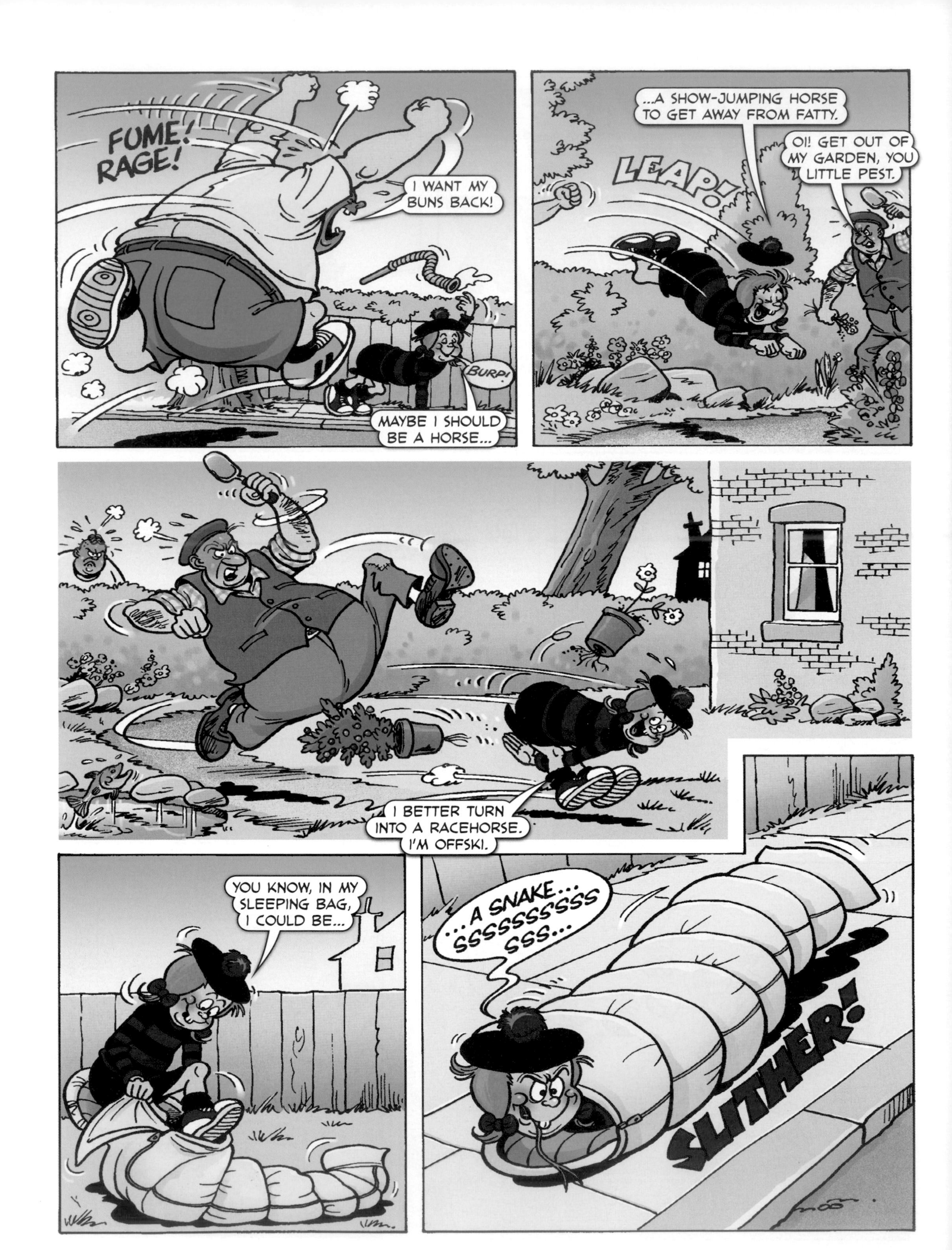
FUME! RAGE!
I WANT MY BUNS BACK!
BURP!
MAYBE I SHOULD BE A HORSE...
...A SHOW-JUMPING HORSE TO GET AWAY FROM FATTY.
LEAP!
OI! GET OUT OF MY GARDEN, YOU LITTLE PEST.
I BETTER TURN INTO A RACEHORSE. I'M OFFSKI.
YOU KNOW, IN MY SLEEPING BAG, I COULD BE...
...A SNAKE... SSSSSSSSSS SSS...
SLITHER!

TRIP!
HISSS!
YIPES. MINNIE! WHAT ARE YOU DOING? I'LL NICK YOU FOR THIS.

YOU WERE SSSSSAYING? USSS SSSSNAKES CAN GIVE YOU A NASSSTY CRUSH.
SLITHER!
OH, ALL RIGHT, I'LL LET YOU GO.

NOW WHAT IS MINNIE BEING?
MINNIE'S GARDEN FENCE.
ME
DEATH-

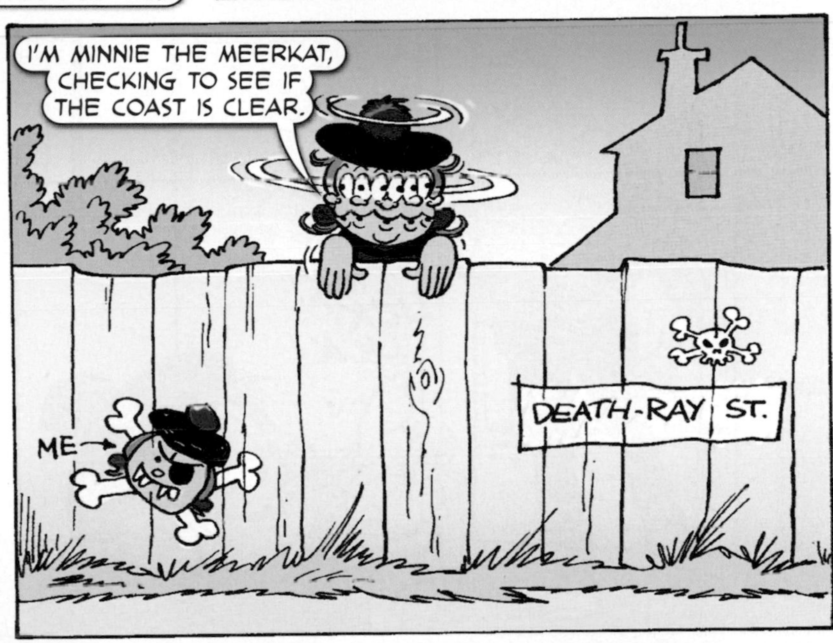
I'M MINNIE THE MEERKAT, CHECKING TO SEE IF THE COAST IS CLEAR.
ME
DEATH-RAY ST.

I'LL GO INTO THE HOUSE THROUGH THE MEERKAT-FLAP.
LOPE!

PUFF!
GRUNT!
PUFF!
?
OORF. IT'S TOO FLAMING SMALL.

SOME D.I.Y. LATER...
THERE! THAT'S MUCH BETTER.
SNIK! SNIK!
CHESTER
NAILS

MAYBE I SHOULD BE A POLAR BEAR...
FREEZER

...COZ I LIKE THE COLD. COLD ICE CREAM ANYWAY.
WHAT'S ALL THIS MONKEY BUSINESS?
LICK! LICK! LICK!

I ALWAYS THOUGHT YOU WERE A LITTLE MONKEY.
HEE-HEE!
SLURP!

AND YOU KNOW WHAT? SHE MAKES A MONKEY OUT OF ME ALL THE TIME.
OOK! OOK! OOK!
GRUNT! GRUNT! GRUNT!
GIRLY STUFF
KEN. H HARRISON.

SILLY SAFARI
CHECK THESE WEIRD ANTARCTIC ANIMALS!
OSTRICH BURYING HEAD IN SNOW.
FEED UVVER END
OINK!
SPLINTER! CRA-ACK!
MAXIMUM LOAD 5 TONS.
GIRAFFE WITH A SORE THROAT.
WANTED!
KRAZY KOALA
SKIING KANGAROO

THE NUMSKULLS
COME ON, GUYS!
MOUTH DEPT.
WE'RE GOING FOR A PICNIC...
THROAT DEPT.
...BY THE SHORES OF EDD'S TUM!
TUM DEPT.
FIZZ
SOON -
THAT WAS GREAT!
WHAT'LL WE DO NOW?
BURP!
BELCH!
PAT! PAT!
FIZZ
TUM DEPT.
I'VE AN IDEA! WE'LL PLAY DUCKS AND DRAKES!
SEE HOW MANY TIMES MY APPLE PIP SKIMMED? SIX!
CHUCK!
TUM JUICE
FLIP! SKIP! SKIM!
YOU GIVE US THE PIP!
WE'LL BEAT THAT!
SKIP!
SKIM!
HURL!

LOOK WHAT'S UNDER THE SURFACE!
SKIP!
OW! GRR!
THUD!
BIFF! BONK!
CLONK!
THROW STONES AT ME, WOULD YOU?
IT'S THE TUMMY BUG!
SPLOSH!
ROARR!
RUN AWAY!
SLOBBER! SLAVER!
SUDDENLY -
I DON'T FEEL VERY WELL!
TOTTER! STAGGER!
I THINK YOU'VE GOT A TUMMY BUG!

SLOBBER! DROOL!
EDD DOES HAVE A TUMMY BUG AND IT WANTS TO EAT NUMSKULL.
MUST DO SOMETHING!
SCREAM!
BRAIN DEPT.
THIS COULD SAVE US.
EAT ICE CREAM!
I'VE AN URGE TO EAT ICE CREAM.
HOPEFULLY THAT ICE CREAM WILL SETTLE YOUR STOMACH!
CHOMF! SLURP!
OVER HERE, LADS!

WE'RE VERY SORRY FOR GETTING YOU ALL HOT AND BOTHERED!
HAVE SOME ICE CREAM!
SCOOP!
SMACK! SLOO!
MM! NICE! SOOTHING!
SUDDENLY -
I FEEL MUCH BETTER NOW!
SO -
STRANGE! THAT TUMMY BUG DIDN'T LAST LONG!
NOD!
FLICK!
MOP!
IF ONLY SHE KNEW THE TRUTH!
GURGLE! BLOOP!
I'LL BE BACK!
-TOM PATERSON-

BILLY WHIZZ
WAHEY! I'M OFF FOR A FEW HUNDRED MILES' JOG! IT'S SUCH A NICE DAY!
WHIZZZZZ
HMM! HERE COMES BILLY NOW.
WHO'S THIS?
NIGEL PARKINSON
SUDDENLY -
WAA!
ONE ... TWO ...
SWOOSH!
WOA! DID I JUST PASS SOMEONE AT WHIZZSPEED?
SCREECH!
DOH! SAVE THIS SPORTS SCIENTIST!
AHEM! I'M SORRY. I WAS MOVING SO FAST - I DIDN'T SEE YOU THERE!

ER ... I WAS TRYING TO STUDY YOUR MOVEMENTS. FIND OUT WHY YOU ARE THE FASTEST BOY IN THE WORLD.
HEH - HEH! YOU SHOULD HAVE JUST ASKED FOR MY HELP.
SO, IN THE LAB -
WOW! WHAT SUPER SPEED!
THIS TEST SHOULD SHOW UP THE SECRET OF BILLY'S SPEED!
X RAY
BUT -
CHORTLE! WHAT'S UP, DOC? DIDN'T FIND THE ANSWER?
SIGH!
NOTHING SPECIAL FOUND
THEN -
MAYBE IT'S SOMETHING TO DO WITH MY DIET! BACK IN A SECOND!
GOOD IDEA, BILLY!
ONE SECOND LATER -
THIS IS MY MUM'S SECRET RECIPE BOOK.
AHA! THERE COULD BE CLUES TO YOUR SPEED IN THERE.

HARE STEW WITH EXTRA RUNNER BEANS
DRINK LOTS OF INSTANT COFFEE
MINUTE STEAKS WITH NANO SECOND BREAD
TRY QUICK SETTING JELLY
HURRY CURRY
NO FASTING THOUGH!
LEMON BALSAMIC CHICKEN WITH SPRING ONIONS
PORK WITH RUNNY HONEY AND LEMON ZEST
ANY FAST FOOD!
TUNA BAKE, SWEET POTATO WITH ROCKET SALAD
BAMBOO SHOOTS WITH BUTTERNUT SQUASH
SCONES MADE WITH SELF-RAISING FLOUR
OLIVE-OIL WITH EVERYTHING WILL GET YOU RUNNING!!
WELL, THE RECIPES SEEMED TO HAVE WORKED FOR THE SCIENTIST. HE COOKED AND TRIED THE FOOD.
BUT EATING IT ALL AT ONCE HAS WORKED PRETTY QUICKLY - ON HIS TUM! CHORTLE!
GENTS LOO
GANGWAY! GOTTA GO! OO ... WAA!
SO, WHY AM I THE FASTEST BOY IN THE WORLD? CHORTLE! IT'S STILL A HUGE MYSTERY! I'M NOT TELLING.
ODD BOFFINS UK

SILLY SAFARI
BLAAT! SQUONK!
OASIS DUCK
DA-DUM... DA-DUM... DA-DUM...
SAND SHARK
BURRP! BELCH!
PICNICING PANDA
COCONUT EATING HAMSTER
WORLD'S BEST CHAMELEON.
FIZZO
BABY RATTLESNAKE
RATTLE! RATTLE!
HITH-TH-THH!

LES PRETEND

VERY EARLY ONE MORNING -
I'M EAGER TO BE UP AND PRETENDING TODAY!

I'M GOING TO BE A BEAVER!

LATER, AT BREAKFAST -
I NEED MY CRUNCHY FLAKES, AND A NICE SIT DOWN.
LES'S DAD.
CRUNCHY FLAKES

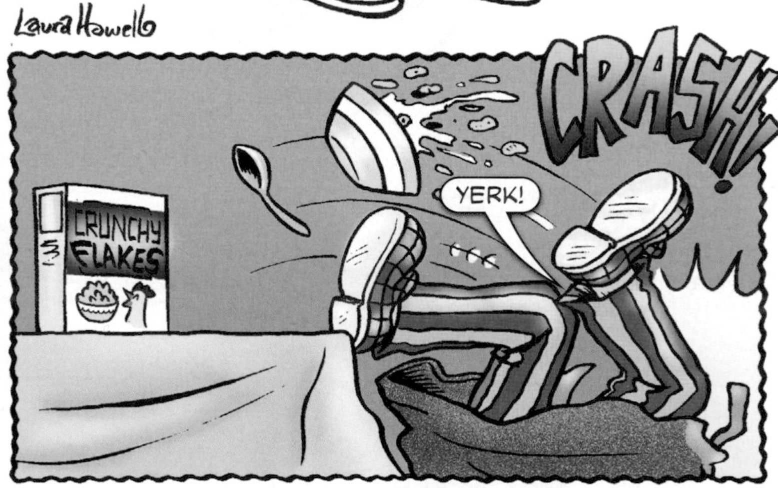
Laura Howell
CRASH!
YERK!
CRUNCHY FLAKES

WE BEAVERS EAT WOOD!

GERROUTOFIT, YOU TOOTHY PEST!

WHAT A SPLENDID SAPLING!

GNAW GNAW GNAW
SOON HAVE IT DOWN.

SHORTLY -

ANOTHER USEFUL TREE.

SOON HAVE ENOUGH FOR MY DAM!

AND -
THAT SHOULD BE STRONG ENOUGH!

NOW TO LET THE RIVER FLOW.

PERFECT BEAVER HABITAT!

NOW THAT I'VE FINISHED BREAKFAST, I'M READY TO FACE THE DAY! I'LL START OFF WITH A BRACING SHOWER.
CREEAK
WHAT THE...?
WAIT TILL I GET MY HANDS ON YOU!
GULP! BETTER BE OFF - MAN HUNTED BEAVERS TO EXTINCTION IN BRITAIN!

SILLY SAFARI
RUSTED SLOTH
CRE-EAK!
SQUEAK!
OIL
SQUIRT!
SICK AS A PARROT
OOG! OOG!
CRICKET BATS
WELLY WEARING TAPIR
SINGING IN THE RAINFOREST
TAPIR EATING PIRANHA

FREDDIE FEAR

HA - HA!
CHEEK! I WANTED TO TAKE MY WITCHING STUFF!
CHUCK!
EVERYTHING BUT THE KITCHEN SINK!

SOON -
WAA! WE'RE OFF!

THE CASTLE'S HIGH ABOVE THE MOUNTAINS.
WITH A GREAT VIEW OF A GRAVEYARD! SMASHING!
FLAP!
FLAP!

BUT THEN -
EH? SHOULDN'T WE BE GOING DOWN TO LAND?
IT'S A REAL CASTLE IN THE SKY, FREDDIE!
SWOOP!

THERE IT IS!
FLAP!
IT REALLY IS FLOATING ON THE CLOUDS! GASP!

THIS IS VERY STRANGE. BUT THEN, NOT SO ODD FOR MY MUM!
LET'S GO INSIDE.

WONDERFUL! RUNNING WATER!
HEH - HEH!
DRIP! PLIP!
ER ... DOWN THE WALLS, MUM!
DRIP GURGLE!
LOTS OF PLANT LIFE.

TOADSTOOLS GROWING ON THE TABLE!
YOUR UNCLE'S WORLD FAMOUS ...
... SKULL COLLECTION! WHAT FUN! HA - HA!
AW! I'M BORED ALREADY.

GO AND PLAY OUTSIDE!
SHOVE!
HUH!

HMM! THE CLOUD'S FLOATING! I WONDER?

I HAVE A PLAN. ALL I NEED IS A LUMP OF COAL ON A STRING.
HERE GOES.
TOSS!
HERE GOES, WHAT?
AND -
IT'S WORKING. WE'RE TOWING THE CASTLE!
TUG!
DRAG!
FLUTTER! FLAP!
SOON -
NOW LET ME SEE ...
...YAHOO! DOWN THROUGH THE CLOUDS WE GO!
DIVE!
DOWN BELOW -
HA - HA! I TOWED THE CASTLE ABOVE A SUNNY BEACH.
SO, UP IN THE CASTLE IN THE CLOUDS -
SIGH! WHAT A WONDERFUL HOLIDAY SPOT!
FASHION GHOUL
AND DOWN BELOW -
THE BEST OF BOTH WORLDS FOR OUR HOLIDAY! CHORTLE! THANKS, DRAGON!
SLURP! YOU'RE WELCOME!
TOM PATERSON

SILLY SAFARI
SPIDER CRAB
PUFF!
PORCUPINE FISH
BANG!
POP!
SWELL!
HAMMERHEAD SHARK
SURFING TURTLE
MOHICLAM

Dennis and GNASHER®
LOOK AT THE TWO OF YOU - SO-OOO MUCKY.

IT WAS WORTH IT TO WIN THE MUD SLALOM THOUGH, GNASHER.

WELL, I'M SPLITTING YOU TWO UP. GNASHER IS GOING TO KEEP GRAN COMPANY WHILE GNIPPER IS AWAY AT PUP CAMP.
YOU CAN'T!
SHE CAN. SORRY, GNASHER. YOU'RE OFF TO GRAN'S.

I'LL COME AND SEE YOU EVERY DAY, GNASHER!

BYE PAL!
GNASH!

HEY, DENNIS. READY FOR THE PET SHOW?
HI CURLY. HI, PIE FACE. NO, I'M NOT READY.

I CAN'T GO TO THE PET SHOW WITHOUT MY HOUND. I NEED GNASHER.

OR I NEED A GNASHER.
SLAM

IN THE TREEHOUSE -
WE NEED A GOOD MENACING PLAN!

AND I'VE JUST HAD ONE!

WANNA PLAY A GAME, BEA? GOOD!

I'LL SACRIFICE MY OLD CUDDLY DOG TOY, DUDLEY!

IN YOU GO, BEA.
BEANO

PRETTY GOOD, EH?

BEANO
AND BEA LIKES CRAWLING ON ALL FOURS.

FRRRAPP!
PITY SHE'S NOT HOUSE TRAINED.

AIR! FRESH AIR!

TIME FOR PLAN D AND G!

'SCUSE ME, DAD. I NEED THE RUG.

NOW I'M GETTING WORRIED!

THEN -
IT FITS LIKE A RUG, P.F.!

ON WITH OVEN GLOVE EARS.
AND WHISKERS!

BEANOTOWN AREN
YOU LOOK GREAT, PIE FACE.
PET SHOW TODAY
FLEA POWDER DEMONSTRATION TONIGHT
SO WHY DO I FEEL DAFT?

THAT'S AN UNUSUAL DOG, DENNIS!
A LESSER SPOTTED PIE HOUND, WALTER.
JUDGE

FIRST UP IS THE OBSTACLE COURSE, DOG OF MINE.
I'M NOT DOING IT!

NOT EVEN FOR A PIE?
YES.

GOOD DOG!

THE PIE IS SO CLOSE.

NOW BEG!

I BELIEVE WE WIN.
I HATE TO SAY IT, BUT WELL DONE.
1ST

THANKS, WALTER.
IT SPOKE!

SO! FAKE EARS!

CHEATING MAKES ME ANGRY!
YOU SHOULDN'T HAVE STOMPED ON THE PIE.

GRRR!
NICE DOG. CALM DOWN.

STOP! THIS IS AGAINST THE RULES!
LET'S GET GNASHER BACK. HE'S LESS TROUBLE.

SPACE CADET SMIFFY
IT'S THE UGLIEST PLANET IN THE UNIVERSE - PLUGO!
ESCAPE HATCH
PLANET JANET WELCOMES CAREFUL WOMEN DRIVERS
2 PINTS PLEASE
MILKY WAY
OUTSIDE TOILET

LORD SNOOTY
NOOTY I
WING COMMANDER SNOOTY
ADMIRAL SNOOTY
THE BARD OF BUNKERTON
NIGEL PARKINSON
BEING AN INCREDIBLY WEALTHY TOFF IS JOLLY SPLENDID AND EVERYTHING...
PARKINSON, THE RELIABLE BUT UNDERPAID BUTLER...

SWIMMING POOL
TENNIS COURTS
SHOWERS
GAMES ROOM
BIG BOX OF BALLS– JUST A BIG BOX OF BALLS
...BUT IT'S NOT SO MUCH FUN FOR SPORTS.

TO YOU, PARKINSON.

WELL PLAYED, SIR. YOUR POINT.
DELIBERATE STEP BACKWARDS

YOUR SHUTTLECOCK, SIR, AND MAY I SUGGEST A PAY-RISE FOR A GOOD LOSER?
YOU DIDN'T EVEN TRY. THAT'S NO FUN AT ALL!

FIFI, THE FRENCH MAID, WHO REALLY IS FRENCH.
AT LEAST PARKINSON IS TRYING AT TABLE TENNIS.
LE WHAT? HE EEZ TRYING? ZE NO!

YOU MUST NOT TRY MONSIEUR PARKINSON. HE EEZ ZE BOSS.
HAPPY CHRISTMAS TO ALL OUR READERS
ESPECIALLY THE VERY RICH ONES.
AAAH... AAAAH...

ZE OH, DEAR. FOUL SHOT. HEEZ LORDSHIP EEZ ZE WINNER.
CHOOO
GOOD SHOT
THIS IS JUST TERRIBLE. THEY WON'T TRY TO BEAT ME AT ANYTHING.

LET ME DIVE OUT OF THE WAY SO YOU GET A BETTER VIEW OF YOUR SPLENDID SHOT GOING IN, SIR.
THEY DON'T EVEN TRY AT FOOTBALL.
WELL PLAYED, SIR. BAD LUCK IN GOAL, TOMPKINSON.

I THOUGHT MY FRIENDS MIGHT ENJOY GETTING THE BETTER OF MY SERVANTS - THEY'RE NOT USED TO THIS TOADYING...

ONE COULD TRY TO GET ONE'S LEGS FURTHER APART TO HELP YOUR NEXT NUTMEG, SIR.
THIS IS BOGUS AND BORING, SNOOTS. THEY'RE NOT EVEN TRYING HERE.
...BUT EVEN MY CHUMS GET TIRED OF IT AFTER A WHILE.
BUT I KNOW HOW TO SORT THESE UNDERSTAIRS TYPES AND GET THEM TRYING...
I'VE BEEN WATCHING YOU ALL PLAYING SPORTS. YOU'RE ALL RUBBISH, SO I'M GIVING YOU..
A PAY-RISE, SIR?
...A 50% PAY-CUT, FOR EMBARRASSING ME AND BUNKERTON CASTLE!
ZE WHAT?
WHAT?
GET HIM!
TAKE THIS!
AFTER ALL ZE CRAWLING WE DID?
I KNEW THEY'D TRY ONCE THEIR DANDERS WERE UP. I'LL TELL THEM THE PAY CUT WAS A GAG LATER!

YOU'VE GOT A SURPRISE FOR US, PATTI?
YEAH - KEEP YOUR EYES COVERED.
HELP!

HEY, YOU'RE CHEATING ON MY BIG SURPRISE.
WELL, WE ARE RATS, YOU KNOW.

RATZ
OPENING TODAY
EVERYONE WELCOME!
BEANOTOWN SHOPPING CENTRE
LOOK AT THIS! WE'VE GOT A NEW SHOPPING CENTRE. I LOVE SHOPS.
Laura Howe/16

WE HATE SHOPPING.

BUT WE LOVE HAVING FUN.

IN
WHY DO I GET THE FEELING THAT THIS WASN'T MY BEST IDEA EVER?
CHAAAAAARGE!

NEW RELEASES
MUSIC MAN
SALE
METAL
WOTCHER, MATE. WE'RE IN FOR CD'S AND DVD'S.

READY, MATE?
I'VE GOT ME ELASTIC BAND!

FLING
TWANG
SPLAT!
PULL! CLAY-PIGEON SHOOTING RATZ-STYLE!
SHOT, KEEF!

LOOK! BOOKS!
Spatula City
Bargain Cave
Shoe Citadel
Lovely Things
Coffee Sir?
Pie Hut
WORLD O' CHEESE
THERE'S SO MANY SHOPS! WHICH ONE DO I CHOOSE?

I'LL CLOSE ME EYES AND PICK ONE!

HELLO, LADY.
UH?

EEKS! A RAT!
EEKS! I'M IN THE WOMEN'S UNDERCRACKERS SHOP!
BIG FRILLY KNICKERS
Sale

AT LEAST THERE'S PARACHUTES I CAN USE TO ESCAPE WIV!

IN FOOD-O-MART...
Juicy Yum
Sunny Mix
TASTY FLAKES
SOME OF THAT, PLENTY OF THAT, SOME OF THIS...
NOM FLAKES
RICE

BIP BIP BIP
BISCUITS... GRAPES...

HALLO, MISSUS. DO YOU TAKE I.O.U.s?
TAKE THE BISCUITS! SCREAM!

HEH-HEH! WE LOVE SHOPPING!
YEAH!
SIGH. I HATE SHOPPING!
OPENING TODAY
EXCEPT RATS!
BEANOTOWN SHOPPING CENTRE

IT'S ALWAYS SUNNY AT THE SUN!
BOOSTER ROCKET PLACE 20p IN SLOT & PRESS BUTTON
SPACE CADET SMIFFY
WOW! THESE MERCURIANS ARE NEARLY AS FAST AS BILLY WHIZZ!
STAND HERE FOR A FAST SUN TAN!
WELCOME TO MERCURY SPEED LIMIT: 10,000 KPH -NO SLOWER!

BALL BOY

HERE'S THIS WEEK'S TEAM, FOLKS.
WHY BOTHER LOOKING?
THE FIRST NAME ON THE SHEET IS ALWAYS 'BALL BOY'.

NOT THIS WEEK - I'VE PUT MYSELF ON THE BENCH SO EVERYBODY ELSE CAN GET A GAME.
TOP MAN!
YAY!

WHAT A GUY! WHAT A GREAT GUY!
WELL, I'M A TEAM PLAYER, ME.

OOH, THE PITCH IS SOAKED AND MUDDY. THAT MEANS...
I'LL BE IN THE DUG-OUT, LADS.
HOME DUG OUT

...SLIDING TACKLES! WAHEEEEEY!
SPLUSH!

I'LL SHOW OUR OPPONENTS A CLEAN PAIR OF HEELS!
SPLURT!
SPLOSH!
SPLISH!
THEY'RE NOT CLEAN! THEY'RE FILTHY MUDDY!
IT'S GREAT WEATHER FOR FLASHY SAVES...
DIVE!
CLUTCH!
WHEEEE!
SPLASH!
...AND SPLASHY SAVES!
I'M TAKING A LONG RUN UP TO THIS NEXT SLIDING TACKLE.
CHAARGE!
IT'LL BE A SNORTER!
LUNGE!
EEKS!
OH, NO. THIS COULD BE TERRIBLE.
WHAT ARE YOU HIDING BEHIND ME FOR? TOO MUCH OF A WIMP TO WATCH A HARD TACKLE?
NOPE.

SPLATTER!
GOT IT!
SLIDE!
BLUG!
JUST TOO SMART TO STAND IN THE WAY OF A MUD-SPRAY.

OKAY, BALL BOY. I'M HERE TO TAKE YOUR TEAM PHOTOGRAPH.
COOL, MR PHOTOGRAPHER.
TEAM PHOTO? BUT WE'RE ALL MUDDY!
ALL EXCEPT BALL BOY - THAT'S WHY HE DIDN'T PLAY TODAY!

THE PHOTOGRAPH

BRILLIANT, EH? WHAT A FANTASTIC PHOTO.
NO IT FLAMING ISN'T, YOU ROTTER! MY MUM WILL HATE THAT PIC! I'M ALL MUDDY!
YOU CALL YOURSELF A TEAM PLAYER?
-TOM PATERSON-

SPLOT!
SPLUT!
WELL, YOU'RE JUST LIKE PART OF THE TEAM NOW.
BLUG!
CHUCK!

WEB WARS

PLATFORM CHALLENGE TODAY - YOU FIRST, BEA!

ME'S TOO SMALL!

PHRRRTT!
SHE MAY BE SMALL, BUT SHE'S JET PROPELLED!

UH, OH, BEA'S BLASTED HERSELF OUT OF THE GAME.

GNASHER'S UP FOR THIS ONE!

AW, NOW HE'S DOWN FOR THIS ONE!

ME NOW - ON TO THE NEXT LEVEL!

BUT -
-10
TEE-HEE! DENNIS DIDN'T SEE MY KITTEN CHIBIE!
-10
-10

AND THE WINNER IS . . . NONE OF US!

DENNIS-IDOKU

Dennis has invented this fiendish 'Dennis-idoku' puzzle – it's sure to keep Mrs Creecher busy while he gets up to some menacing!

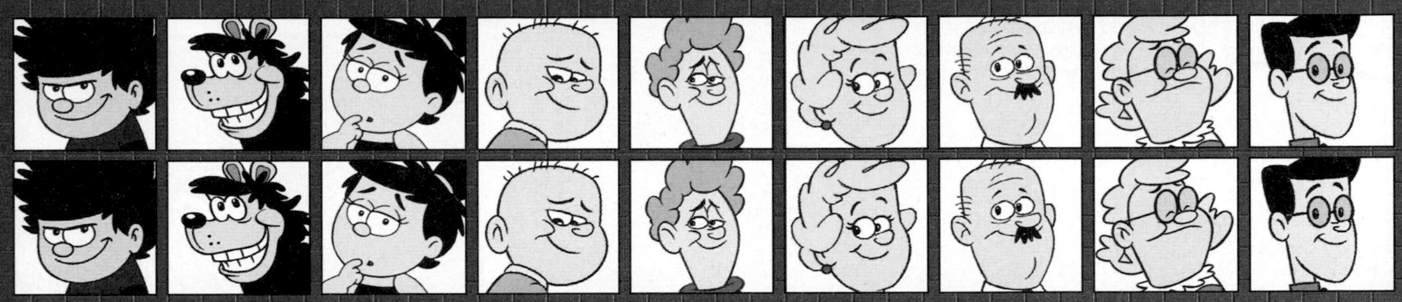

The 18 squares below all fit into the grid – but remember, each character can fit in each row only ONCE both across and down the way.

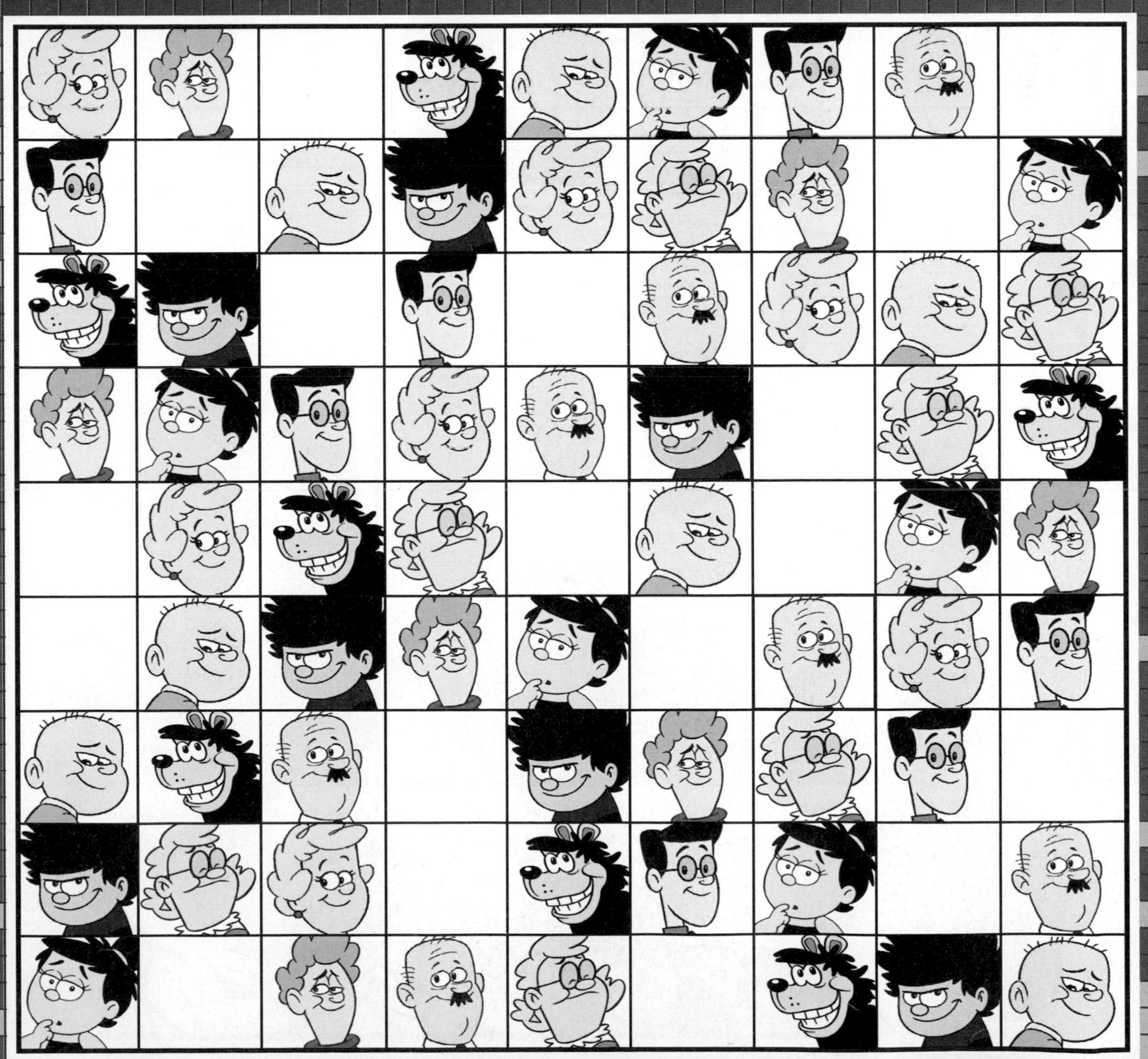

Schoolchildren William and Kathleen Grange lead a secret life as costumed crime fighters...
BILLY the CAT and Katie
But even heroes have to take a holiday sometimes...
Greetings from Windburn-on-Sea
WISH YOU WERE HERE
Nigel Dobbyn 09
WISH I WASN'T!
GIVE IT A CHANCE. MUM'S BEEN LOOKING FORWARD TO VISITING AUNTY BERYL FOR AGES.
BUT THIS PLACE IS SO BORING.
YOU MEAN THERE'S NO CRIME TO FIGHT.
HONESTLY, I DON'T THINK YOU KNOW HOW TO RELAX -
I'M SURPRISED YOU DIDN'T BRING YOUR COSTUME WITH YOU.
UM, WELL...
YOU DIDN'T.
NEVER LEAVE HOME WITHOUT IT!

WILLIAM, KATHLEEN... BERYL AND I ARE GOING TO FIND SOMEWHERE FOR LUNCH AND THEN MAYBE CHECK OUT THE BINGO. DO YOU WANT TO COME?
OKAY, MUM.
BINGO? I DON'T THINK SO!
UM, I'M GOING TO HEAD INTO TOWN... SEE WHAT'S GOING ON THERE.
SEE YOU...
...WOULDN'T WANNA BE YOU!
One quick costume change later...
THERE MUST BE SOMEONE CAUSING TROUBLE IN THIS DEAD END TOWN.
ALL I'VE GOT TO DO IS WAIT...
Later still...
AND WAIT...
EEEEEEEEEEK!
AT LAST!
ACTION!

MY PURSE! HE'S STOLEN MY PURSE!
WHAT THE...?
YOU MIGHT AS WELL GIVE UP. YOU CAN'T GET AWAY FROM ME...
KLAK!
...OWWW!
ROOOARRRR!
OH YEAH? SAYS WHO?

Meanwhile, Katie is having problems of her own...
Lunchtime KARAOKE today
MAMMA MIA, HERE I GO AGAIN...
I AM SO ASHAMED!

MAYBE BILLY HAD THE RIGHT IDEA AFTER ALL.
Amusements
DRINKS
I WONDER WHERE HE'S HANGING AROUND.

WAAAAH!
TALK ABOUT 'NOT ENOUGH ROOM TO SWING A CAT'!
IF ONLY I COULD GET MY FEET ON THE GROUND I COULD....

WOOOAH!

IT'S *NO USE,* I'M GOING TO HAVE TO LET THIS CREEP *GO!*
SLASH!
I GUESS THAT'S YOU DOWN TO *EIGHT LIVES,* CAT BOY!

LOOKS LIKE HE'S HEADING TOWARDS THE *SEA FRONT.*
I'LL HAVE TO TRY AND TRACK HIM DOWN *THERE.*

Back at the *amusement arcade...*
I HATE TO ADMIT BILLY'S *RIGHT,* BUT THIS PLACE *ISN'T* VERY...

OOOOFF!
OWWW!
...INTERESTING!
I'M *SO SORRY.* ARE YOU ALRIGHT?
I'M *FINE,* DON'T WORRY. NOTHING HURT BUT MY *PRIDE,* AS THEY SAY.
IN *THAT* CASE, MAYBE I COULD BUY YOUR *PRIDE* AN *ICE CREAM* TO MAKE IT *FEEL BETTER?*
Willie

Amusements
MY NAME'S *JOSH,* BY THE WAY.
THAT *RED MOTORCYCLE HELMET - GOT* YOU!
WITH... *KATIE?*

I KNOW IT WAS YOU. GIVE ME BACK THAT PURSE YOU STOLE.
W...WHAT? I...I DON'T KNOW WHAT YOU'RE TALKING ABOUT.
ARE YOU SUPPOSED TO BE A GOTH OR SOMETHING?
WHAT IS YOUR PROBLEM, BILLY?
THIS GUYS A THIEF. I'VE JUST CHASED HIM FROM TOWN. HE HAD THIS ROCKET POWERED SKATEBOARD HE WAS USING.
AND WHERE'S THIS SUPPOSED SKATEBOARD?
UH, WELL, HE'S OBVIOUSLY STASHED IT SOMEWHERE.
YOU SAW HIS FACE?
WELL, NO, HE WAS WEARING THAT HELMET, BUT...
THAT'S ENOUGH, BILLY. JUST BECAUSE YOU'RE HAVING A ROTTEN TIME, DOESN'T MEAN YOU HAVE TO RUIN EVERYONE ELSE'S.
BUT...
COME ON, JOSH. I SEEM TO REMEMBER YOU PROMISED TO BUY ME AN ICE CREAM?
DO YOU KNOW THAT GUY?
NO... NO I DO NOT.
WHY ON EARTH WOULD I HANG AROUND WITH A LOSER LIKE THAT?
Is this the end of Billy and Katie's partnership? Find out in Part Two, later on!

FIENDS REUNITED

SWIPE!
OOH, TA VERY MUCH!
WAAAGH!
FOR YOU!
TA!
KRAK!
ALGIE! HOW ARE YOU?
GERVAISE! HAVEN'T SEEN YOU IN AGES! HOW'S THE WIFE?
BINKY, YOU CHAPS WERE INVITED TOO! FANCY SEEING YOU HERE!
I WONDER WHO INVITED US?
THE POSTMAN?
NOT JUST THE POSTMAN...

FWIP!
IT IS I, DOCTOR FRANKENSTEIN, YOUR CREATOR!
SO IT IS! HAVEN'T SEEN HIM SINCE...

SINCE YOU ALL ESCAPED FROM MY LAB MANY YEARS AGO.
WE DIDN'T ESCAPE - WE JUST MOVED OUT. LIVE WITH IT.

WELL, I'VE MOVED ON. TO SHOW THERE'S NO HARD FEELINGS, MEET MY LATEST CREATION...
...FRANKENSWINE!
EEKS!
HOW DO WE GET OUT?
GRUNT!
SNORK!
CRASH!
OH, DEAR. I'D BETTER PUT THEM BACK TOGETHER.
I DO HOPE I'VE GOT THIS RIGHT...
OOH, NO! IT'S LOVELY.
WE REALLY ARE FIENDS REUNITED, AREN'T WE?
WE CAN HAVE A PROPER CHINWAG!
NOPE. BACK TO THE DRAWING BOARD.
NICK BRENNAN

BANANAGIRL: LIKE BANANAMAN, - ONLY SHORTER!
SAFARI SAM: CAN CHANGE INTO ANY ANIMAL!
STINKBOMB: SUPER-SMELLY!
INVISIBLE ISOBEL: SHE CAN DISAPPEAR!
WATERBOY: HE CONTROLS WATER!
SUPER SCHOOL
HEY, IT'S ALL CLOUDY OUTSIDE.
SCHOOL RULE Nº 612: DO NOT PUT OLD SOCKS IN SIR'S SANDWICHES
RATZ
PAPERS TO MARK
SIR'S CHAIR KEEP OFF
OOPS! I'M ON THE WRONG PAGE!
WEIRD. THE FORECAST SAID IT WAS GOING TO BE SUNNY TODAY.
EEKS! I DON'T LIKE LIGHTNING.
OH, PIFFLE. IT'S NOTHING TO WORRY ABOUT, STINKBOMB.
BOOOM!
EEPS! I'M DEAD SCARED OF THUNDER, THOUGH.
PATHETIC.
MWAH-HAH-HAAA!
AM I SUPER-THICK OR DID THAT CLOUD JUST CACKLE?
I HEARD IT TOO. I THOUGHT MY SUPER-IMAGINATION WAS RUNNING WILD.
1

I AM DARK RAIN, THE SUPER-VILLAIN, AND THIS SCHOOL BELONGS TO ME! MWAH-HAH-HAH!
DARK RAIN? WHAT SORT OF DAFT NAME IS THAT?

OKAY. FORGET I SAID THAT. HE TURNS THE RAIN DARK.
HE'S NOT THE ONLY ONE WHO CAN CONTROL WATER...

I'LL SHOW HIM!
SILLY BOY. I DON'T JUST CONTROL WATER...

FREEZE!
... I CONTROL...

...ALL OF THE WEATHER AS WELL.
BUMS.
NEVER BE WITHOUT A BEANO

NOW I SHALL RULE THE WORLD. MWHAH-HAH-HAH!
I'M BANANAGIRL BUT HE'S COMPLETELY BANANAS. LET'S SORT HIM OUT!
FEED THREE TIMES A DAY

WHOOSH!
I'M GONNA GET YOU!
REALLY?

NOTHING IN THE WORLD CAN STOP ME NOW!
GUST!
WE'RE DOOMED. DOOMED, DOOMED, DOOMED!
THRRUPP!
STINKBOMB!
A CRAZY VILLAIN IS BAD ENOUGH WITHOUT YOUR BUM GOING LOOPY TOO!
I'M NERVOUS, OKAY?
AWK.

OH, THAT'S NOT RIGHT - THERE'S SOMETHING WRONG WITH HIM. THAT'S WORSE THAN THE ONE HE DROPPED IN THE DINNER QUEUE LAST WEEK. PUT ME OFF MY TOFFEE PUDDING, IT DID.
HOW DID YOU KNOW ABOUT THAT?
ONLY ONE PERSON HAD TOFFEE PUDDING THAT DAY...
ME AND MY BIG MOUTH!

CHANGE!
I KNEW IT! METEOROLOGY BOY - YOU'VE GONE BAD!

CAN YOU BLAME ME? METEOROLOGY BOY IS A RUBBISH NAME. AND CONTROLLING THE WEATHER IS A ROTTEN SUPER-POWER.
GLOOM
YEAH, YEAH. BOO-HOO, POOR YOU. TRY HAVING FARTING AS YOUR POWER, MATE - NOW THAT STINKS!

DEARIE ME - ONE OF MY PUPILS GOING BAD - IT'S DETENTION FOR YOU.
SUPERVILLAINS ALWAYS WIND UP IN THE NICK.
HEADMASTER
HOW ABOUT COMMUNITY SERVICE INSTEAD, SIR?
OOH, CONTROLLING THE WEATHER ISN'T SO BAD AFTER ALL. YAY.
SCIENCE CLASS
SUPER SCHOOL
WARM RAIN
BLOW!
HE'S GIVING EVERYONE THE WEATHER THEY WANT.
BRAINYPAWS: SUPER-INTELLIGENT SCHOOL CAT
DRY YOUR WASHING HERE! ENVIRONMENTALLY FRIENDLY!
PAINT
AND THE WORLD IS SAVED - BY MY FARTING AND A STICKY TOFFEE PUDDING!
JUICE
BEANO
JUICE
LEW STRINGER

IVY THE TERRIBLE

I'M PLAYING OGRES AGAINST NICE PEOPLE!!

AND THE OGRES WIN.

THAT WAS A GOOD GAME. NEED SOMETHING ELSE TO DO.

COO! A CAMERA CREW!

AH! ONE OF OUR LITTLE PEOPLE.
WARDROBE
LORD OF THE THINGS
DAVE EASTBURY

GET INTO COSTUME.
I'M NOT DRESSING UP . . .

OH, YES I AM!

BRILLIANT! I'M AN OGRE WARRIOR!

NOW FOR THE SCENE WHERE THE PRINCE DEFEATS THE GOBLIN.

OUT OF MY WAY, UGLY GOBLIN!

I'M NOT A GOBLIN, I'M A TERRIBLE!

OOF!
TAKE THAT!

YOU CAN'T HIT OUR STAR!

ARRGH!
WHACK!
YEAH? WHO SEZ?

GRR! GET OUT OF OUR MOVIE.

AN' HAVE YOUR STUPID COSTUME BACK!

BEEN OUT PLAYING, IVY?
SLAM!
I WASN'T PLAYING. I FOUGHT A MAGIC PRINCE!
WHAT A BIG IMAGINATION FOR ONE LITTLE GIRL!

ROGER the DODGER
LOOK AT THE DATE!
DEC. 31st.
IT'S NEARLY THE END OF THE YEAR AND THERE ARE PEOPLE I HAVEN'T DODGED YET!
DANNY
FATTY
SPOTTY
SMIFFY
PLUG
BEST GET CRACKING.
DANNY'S GOT A NEW BIKE.
DISGUISE ON!
STOP!
WHAT IS IT?
SKREECH!
I'VE SPOTTED A WOBBLY WHEEL NUT...

...ANY SECOND AND YOU COULD HAVE LOST A WHEEL!
THANKS!
I'D BETTER TEST IT FOR YOU.
BAH! DODGERED! HE JUST WANTED A GO ON MY NEW BIKE!
VROOM!
GOT YOU, DANNY!

LATER -
FATTY NEXT!

NOPE, I DON'T THINK SO!
YOU DON'T THINK WHAT?

A BOY YOUR SIZE COULD NEVER DO A HANDSTAND.
REALLY? WHAT A CHEEK!

WATCH THIS!

I'LL TAKE THAT!

BAH! DODGED!

DELISH!

THERE'S PLUG - HE'S ON MY LIST TOO!

SORRY TO TROUBLE YOU, PLUG, BUT YOU'RE MY FAVOURITE OF ALL THE BASH STREET KIDS!
THAT'S HARDLY A SURPRISE!

WOULD YOU MIND SIGNING YOUR AUTOGRAPH?

NO TROUBLE!
THANKS EVER SO!

GREAT DODGE THAT ONE!

THIS IS WHAT HE ACTUALLY SIGNED!
Mr. Newsagent, Please hand over my copy of this week's Beano to my pal, Roger! Plug
SPOTTY'S TURN NEXT!
I'VE GOT A MIRACLE CURE FOR SPOTS - ONLY £5!
LET ME TRY BEFORE I BUY!
SPLODGE!
LOOK!
WOW! I'LL TAKE IT!
THE OLD MAYONNAISE AND FAKE MIRROR DODGE!
THAT JUST LEAVES SMIFFY TO DODGE.
HI, ROGER! I'M EATING GRASS TO SEE WHAT IT'S LIKE TO BE A HORSE!
THIS IS MY CHANCE!
IF YOU REALLY WANT TO KNOW WHAT IT'S LIKE TO BE A HORSE, YOU COULD GIVE ME A RIDE HOME.
NEIGH BOTHER!
I SUPPOSE THIS COUNTS AS A DODGE!

SHRIEK!
HELLO, FELLOW HORSES!
WE'D LIKE A WORD WITH YOU!
WE TOLD SMIFFY WHAT YOU'D BEEN UP TO AND HE CAME UP WITH A PLAN!
HE MAY BE DAFT BUT HE'S NOT STUPID!
G-GULP!
PREPARE TO FACE A FIRING SQUAD!
SPLAD!
OOOOSH!
RRIP!
GROAN! THE BASH STREET KIDS ARE OFF MY DODGING LIST PERMANENTLY!

GENERAL JUMBO
JUMBO JOHNSON HAS CONTROL OVER HIS VERY OWN MODEL TROOPS.

SPECIAL MISSION TODAY, ALL UNITS. JUST OVER THIS WALL.

JUMBO CONTROLLED HIS OWN FLEET OF HELICOPTERS.

HERE ARE MY SPECIAL FORCES.

CAREFUL AS YOU GO. THIS IS A DANGEROUS MISSION.
STEVE BECKETT

SUDDENLY, ONE OF JUMBO'S SOLDIERS WAS TRAPPED.

ARMED WITH A HIGH PRESSURE WATER GUN, JUMBO'S SOLDIERS CAME TO THE RESCUE.
SOON THE MISSION WAS IN FULL SWING.
JUMBO'S HEADMASTER WAS QUICK TO THANK HIM.
DINCHESTER SECONDARY SCHOOL
THANKS FOR CLEARING THAT OLD CHEWING GUM FROM THE PLAYGROUND. IT'S A NUISANCE.
ANOTHER SUCCESSFUL MISSION COMPLETED.
NOT QUITE COMPLETED.
HOI, YOU. DON'T DROP THAT GUM, BIN IT!

BILLY the CAT and Katie
WISH YOU WERE HERE
Part Two
I HATE SPYING ON KATIE LIKE THIS, BUT I'M SURE THAT CREEP SHE'S GOING OUT WITH IS THE THIEF I'M AFTER.
THE TELESCOPIC VISOR IN MY HELMET WILL HELP ME KEEP TABS ON THEM.
WHAT ARE THEY...?
OH, GROSS! THAT IS NOT SOMETHING I WANT TO SEE!
THAT'S IT. I'M TURNING IN FOR THE NIGHT.
Next morning, at Beryl's house...
MORNING. ISN'T KATHLEEN UP YET?
OH, SHE'S ALREADY GONE OUT, DEAR, WITH HER FRIEND JOSHUA.
HE SEEMS LIKE A NICE LAD, DOESN'T HE, MABEL?
...LIVE IN THE CENTRE OF WINDBURN-ON-SEA, WHERE THE MYSTERIOUS 'SKATER BOY' THIEF HAS JUST STRUCK AGAIN...
WILLIAM, WHERE ARE YOU GOING? WHAT ABOUT YOUR BREAKFAST?
SORRY, AUNT MABEL, I JUST REMEMBERED I HAVE TO MEET SOMEONE.
HONESTLY, MABEL, YOUR WILLIAM'S LIKE A CAT ON A HOT TIN ROOF SOMETIMES!

BILLY? WHAT DO YOU WANT?
IS JOSH STILL WITH YOU, KATIE?
BREEP BREEP
BILLY
IF JOSH IS WITH KATIE, I GUESS HE CAN'T BE THE THIEF. MAYBE I WAS WRONG.
NO, HE HAD TO GO RUN AN ERRAND.
WHY?
I KNEW IT!
BILLY, I'VE TOLD YOU. IT'S NOT...
SKATER BOY'S AT IT AGAIN IN THE TOWN CENTRE.
OKAY, OKAY.
WELL, HOW ABOUT YOU HELP ME CATCH THIS GUY, WHOEVER HE IS?
I'VE GOT YOUR COSTUME HERE.
KATIE...?
UNBELIEVABLE.
FINE!... IF ONLY TO PROVE TO YOU HOW WRONG YOU ARE!
WE'LL SEE...

THERE HE IS. YOU REMEMBER THE PLAN?
OBVIOUSLY...
OKAY THEN...
LET'S DO IT!
YOU AGAIN? HAVEN'T YOU LEARNT YOUR LESSON YET?
I GUESS YOU'RE NOT MUCH OF A TEACHER!

WOOAH!
GOING MY WAY?

AAAAH!
OR MINE?

JUST LIKE HERDING SHEEP!
HARBOUR WALL, SKATER BOY. THERE'S NOWHERE TO GO FROM HERE!

NOT FOR YOU, MAYBE...
BOAT TRIPS
around
Windburn
Harbour

SEE YOU ON THE *OTHER* SIDE....
...NOT!
ROOOARRRR!

NO!

OOOOF!
NO! WHAT ARE YOU *DOING?*
WE'RE TOO *HEAVY!*
WE'RE GOING TO...

SPLAAASH!!

BILLY? *BILLY!*

PTOOO! YUCK!
IF THIS COSTUME *SHRINKS,* I'M SENDING YOU THE *BILL!*
NOW TO SEE WHO YOU *REALLY ARE!*

BUT... BUT...
WHAT'S THE MATTER? CAT GOT YOUR TONGUE?
YOU'RE NOT JOSH!
I TOLD YOU, DIDN'T I?
LOOK, THERE HE IS NOW, WITH THAT...
...OTHER GIRL.
'ERE, MISS, YOU DON'T WANT THAT. THAT'S JUST A LOAD OF OLD FISH GUTS.
I KNOW.
SEE, I KNEW THERE WAS SOMETHING...
DON'T YOU DARE SAY IT.
...FISHY ABOUT HIM!
END

LORD SNOOTY
I WANT TO GO ICE SKATING ON LAKE SNOOTY.
BUT IT'S TOO HOT, SNOOTS.
LAKE SNOOTY
SNOOTY VIEW FOR LORDS ONLY.
NIGEL PARKINSON
THAT'S NOT A PROBLEM. THIS GIANT ICE-MAKING MACHINE WILL FREEZE THE LAKE FOR ME.
HOW MUCH DOES THAT THING COST?
A FEW MILLION - JUST POCKET CHANGE, REALLY.
HE'S GOT BIG POCKETS.
THERE. JUST WHAT I WANTED. ICE SKATING...
BUT I DIDN'T ASK FOR SINKING!
YOU CAN'T BEAT NATURE, SNOOTS. THE SUN'S TOO HOT.
I CAN'T GET SOAKED! I'M RICH! DOESN'T THIS WATER KNOW WHO I AM?
THERE'S ONLY ONE THING FOR IT. PARKINSON! BREAK OUT THE BUNKERTON SPARKLER!
THIS IS NO TIME FOR FIREWORKS!

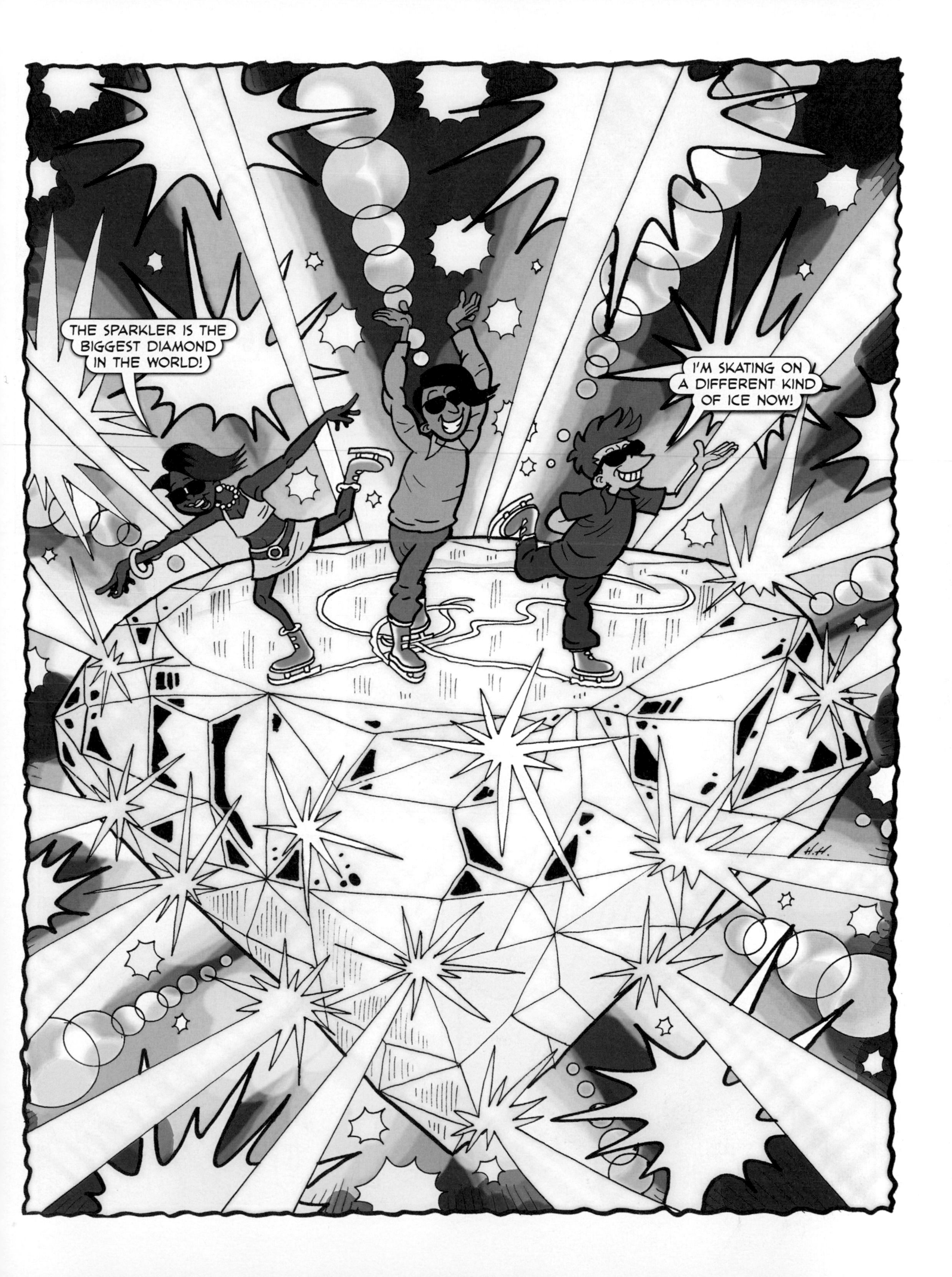
THE SPARKLER IS THE BIGGEST DIAMOND IN THE WORLD!
I'M SKATING ON A DIFFERENT KIND OF ICE NOW!
H.H.

MINNIE THE MINX
HELLO, FOLKS. THINGS ARE ABOUT TO GET VERY WEIRD HERE...

RUMBLE!

FLASH!
FLASH!

DING-DING-
DING-DING!

SMACK!

DO YOU WANT TO KNOW WHAT THIS IS ALL ABOUT?
HAVE YOU WORKED IT OUT YET?

10 200
YOUR SCORE
YOUR SCORE
10
10
5
20
20
9
100
SHORT CUT TO SCHOOL
1000
1000
DOUBLE UP
5
MINNIE LIKES PLAYING PINBALL ON THE COMPUTER SO MUCH...
...THAT MY DAD MADE ME A PROPER PINBALL MACHINE!
KEN.H.HARRISON

A DAY IN THE LIFE OF THE BEANO OFFICE

BEWARE! YOU ARE NOW ENTERING THE BEANO ROOM

MEET THE BEANO OFFICE BOY -
MORNING, EVERY . . .

. . . NO-ONE. THEY'RE ALL LATE TODAY.

EXCEPT FOR DAVE, THE OFFICE CAT. OFF MY SEAT, PUSS.

IT'S BARRY, THE ARTIST.
YO, ALL!
PLOP!

HERE'S LAURA, THE SECRETARY.

I'LL START MY DIET TOMORROW.
HMM. HERE'S A STORY ABOUT A MONKEY THAT DOES YOUR SHOPPING.

FREE GIFTS FOR TESTING!

WOW! THIS ROCKET WOULD BE A GOOD GIFT!

I CAN'T HEAR YOU. I'VE GOT A ROCKET IN MY EAR.

TIME FOR A TEA BREAK. LOVELY.
PTHOO!
DID ANYONE PICK UP THE OLD ENGINE OIL FROM MY MOTOR BIKE? I LEFT IT IN A GLASS.
SORRY, CAN'T HEAR YOU. I'VE GOT OIL IN MY EAR.
SCRIPT CONFERENCE, EVERYONE. I NEED A BASH STREET KIDS STORY.
WHAT IF THE KIDS HAD A FOOD FIGHT IN THE DINNER HALL?

LIKE THIS?
SPLOT!
BLAT!
FLOUR

SPLAT!
MILK
THONK!

YEAH. THAT'LL BE A GOOD STORY.
CAN'T HEAR YOU - I'VE GOT CUSTARD IN MY EAR.
IT'S THE EDITOR!
BEWARE YOU ARE NOW ENTERING THE BEANO ROOM
SORRY I'M LATE, LOT OF TRAFFIC ON THE GOLF COURSE. ANY STORIES FOR ME?
YEAH. A BASH STREET KIDS STORY ABOUT A GIANT FOOD FIGHT.
SEND IT TO THE ARTIST.
ANOTHER BUSY DAY.
THE EDITOR'S GONE. WE'RE OFF HOME!
AH, WELL. TOMORROW'S ANOTHER DAY IN THE BEANO ROOM.

BEANO MANGA (ビーノマンガ)

DENNIS CHIPI IS FEELING HUNGRY.

!

Laura Howell

TWANG

GOTCHA! CAPTURED BY THE BASH STREET CHIPIS.
IN THERE BESIDE THE MINXES AND THE DODGERS!
FLING
HA HA HA HA HA HA!
BASH STREET CHIPIS WIN AGAIN.
PSST! MONKEY!

NOW RETURN THE FAVOUR. GRAB THAT SHINY THING.
OOK? OOK?
IF 'OOK' MEANS 'KEY', THAT'S IT!
HAR! STUPID MENACES AND MINXES.
STUPID, EH?
THE MENACES MADE MONKEYS OF YOU LOT!

THE BASH STREET KIDS
THE KIDS ARE NEVER IN A HURRY TO GET TO SCHOOL.
YAHOO!
HO - HO!
SLOBBER!
MEOW!
OOF!
UNLIKE THEIR TEACHER!
CHORTLE! I CAN'T WAIT TO GET TO SCHOOL!
WOW!
ZOOM
EEK!
SCHOOL
BUSY! BUSY!
ZIP!
HA - HA! WHAT DOES HE MEAN - BUSY? WE'RE NOT IN CLASS YET!
SCHOOL
AAAARGH!
GASP! WHAT'S GOING ON?
DOH!
I RESIGN TEACHER
STAGGER
'BYEE FOREVER, KIDS! I'M OFF!
ZOOM
EH? WHAT DOES TEACHER MEAN BY THAT?

ARE YOU REALLY LEAVING BASH STREET SCHOOL?
YES! I'VE JUST BEEN GIVEN A COPY OF MY LATE UNCLE TAVISH McTEACHER'S WILL. HE'S LEFT ME HIS CASTLE UP IN SCOTLAND! I'M GOING THERE NOW!

NO TEACHER TO TEACH US SO - WE'LL COME WITH YOU!
ER ... OKAY.

GRR! NEVER DARKEN THESE DOORS AGAIN, TEACHER!
GREAT! NEXT STOP SCOTLAND!
PHUT! PHUT!
CLANG!
NUT

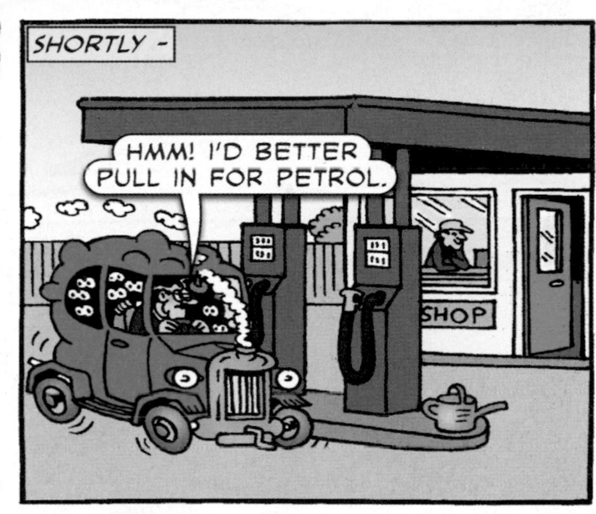
SHORTLY -
HMM! I'D BETTER PULL IN FOR PETROL.
SHOP

GURGLE!
NUT
LET'S GO AND STRETCH OUR LEGS, KIDS.

THEN -
GASP! A HUGE BILL! THE TANK IN MY LITTLE CAR COULDN'T HOLD THAT MUCH PETROL!
ROAD MAPS TO
ROAD MAPS FROM

CHOC
GUM
SWEETS
TOFFEES
MINTS
CRISPS
HA - HA! IT'S THE AMOUNT OF SNACKS FOR THE KIDS WHICH HAS PUSHED UP THE BILL!
DON'T WORRY, SIR. YOU'RE A RICH CASTLE OWNER NOW!
THEN -
HAH! THERE'S SCOTLAND!
SCOTLAND
STOP!
GASP! WHAT NOW?
SHORTLY -
AUCHINTOOGLEMACSHOOGLE
IT'S NOT FAR FROM HERE. WE CAN WALK THE REST OF THE WAY.
LOOK! A LAKE!
A LOCH, PLUG! LAKES ARE LOCHS IN SCOTLAND. HA - HA!

DEEP BELOW IN THE LOCH.
GRR! DID THAT HUMAN JUST CALL ME 'UGLY'?

SNARL! I'LL SHOW THEM!

WOW! WHAT'S THAT?

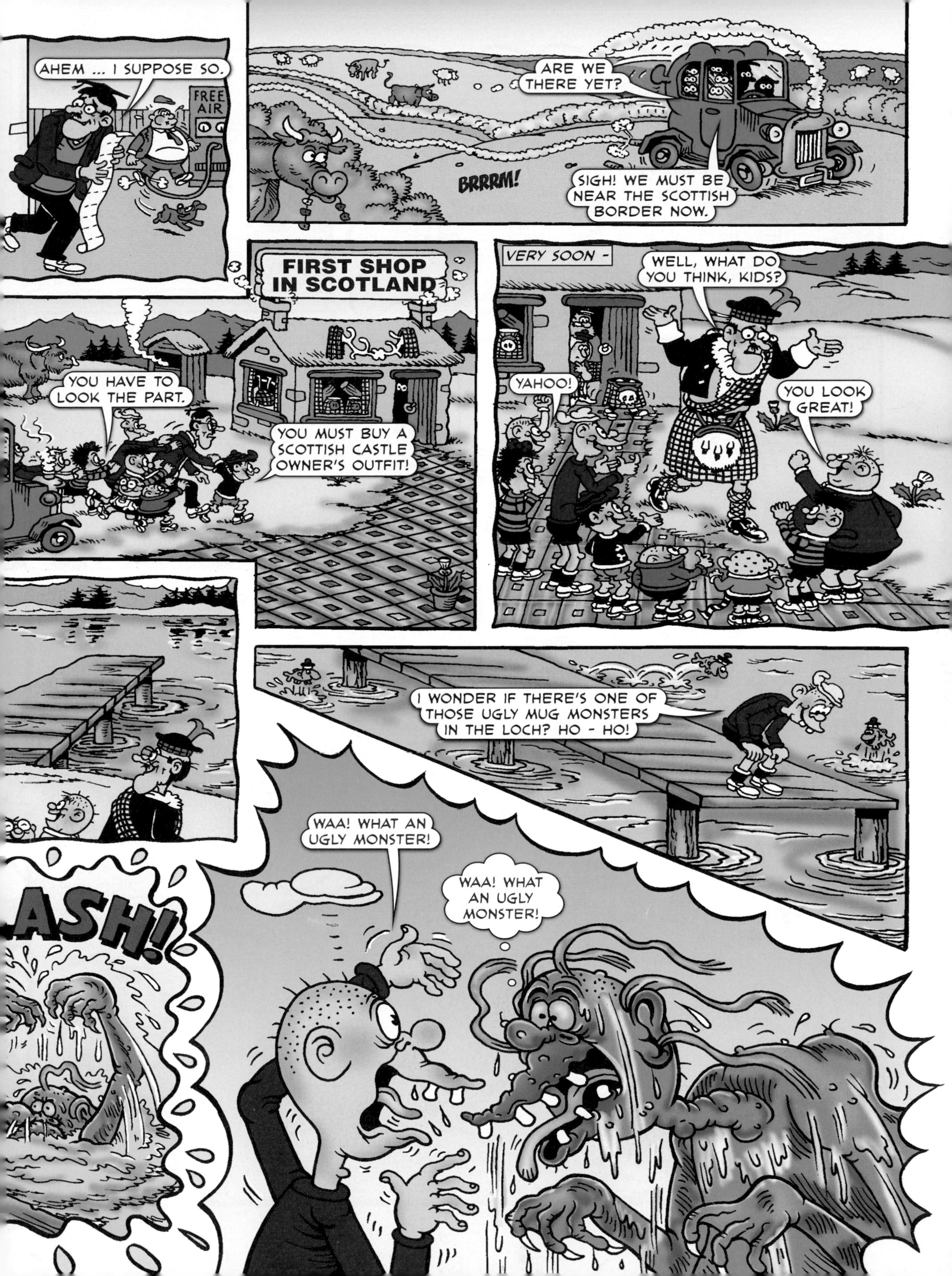
AHEM ... I SUPPOSE SO.
FREE AIR
ARE WE THERE YET?
BRRRM!
SIGH! WE MUST BE NEAR THE SCOTTISH BORDER NOW.
FIRST SHOP IN SCOTLAND
YOU HAVE TO LOOK THE PART.
YOU MUST BUY A SCOTTISH CASTLE OWNER'S OUTFIT!
VERY SOON -
WELL, WHAT DO YOU THINK, KIDS?
YAHOO!
YOU LOOK GREAT!
I WONDER IF THERE'S ONE OF THOSE UGLY MUG MONSTERS IN THE LOCH? HO - HO!
ASH!
WAA! WHAT AN UGLY MONSTER!
WAA! WHAT AN UGLY MONSTER!

SPLASH!
OOOH! THE MONSTER OF THE LOCH! VERY UGLY! HELP!
EEK! I'M NEVER COMING TO THE SURFACE AGAIN!
GIBBER ... MONSTER ... OOOH!
STAGGER
THEN -
SIR, WOULD YOU KNOW WHERE THE CASTLE ONCE OWNED BY MY UNCLE TAVISH McTEACHER MIGHT BE?
HOOTS! AYE! YONDER CASTLE!
WOW! IT'S REAL!
LET'S GO!
BUT -
GGGGASSSPPP!
CHUCKLE!
YAHOO! I DON'T KNOW WHY TEACHER'S SO GLUM. IT MUST BE GREAT TO OWN - A BOUNCY CASTLE! CHUCKLE!
WAHEY!
CABERS
FREE PORRIDGE
PYOING!
HAGGIS
I RESIGN TEACHER
SIMPER! I'LL HAVE TO GO BACK TO FACE HEADMASTER AND CRAWL TO GET MY OLD JOB BACK! SIGH!
DS

Dennis and Gnasher
LOO BRUSH PLEASE, GNASHER!
THANK YOU!
THAT COMPLETES OUR COLONEL SNOWMAN!
HO-HO! VERY LIFELIKE!
TUT-TUT! WHAT A WASTE OF TIME!
WHY DON'T YOU BOYS MAKE YOURSELVES USEFUL AND CLEAR THE SNOW OFF THE DRIVE?
TIME FOR PLAN 'D'!
PESTS!
HEAD FOR THE HILLS!

ON TOP OF A NEARBY HILL -
THESE SPADES WILL MAKE GREAT SLEDGES!

LET'S HAVE A RACE!

OFF WE GO!

GREAT FUN!
I WIN!

MANY RACES LATER!
LET'S MEET UP AGAIN TOMORROW!
YEAH! THAT WAS TERRIFIC!

NEXT MORNING -
CAN'T WAIT FOR ANOTHER DAY'S PLAY IN THE SNOW.

GASP! I DON'T BELIEVE IT!

THERE'S BEEN A THAW! THE SNOW'S MELTED!

WHAT'LL WE DO WITHOUT THE SNOW?
I'VE GOT AN IDEA - FOLLOW ME!
WE'LL BORROW THE SNOW-MAKING MACHINE FROM THE ARTIFICIAL SKI SLOPE!
THE GUY THAT WORKS HERE IS A PAL OF MINE.
TODAY, I THINK WE'LL MAKE A MRS CREECHER SNOW-WOMAN!
ON IT GOES.
CLICK!
SORRY, GUYS!
PH!
SOON -
THIS IS AWESOME!

WHEN DO YOU THINK WE'LL HAVE ENOUGH?
ABOUT NOW!

I'VE BROKEN THE SWITCH - THIS CAN'T BE GOOD!

EVEN GIVING IT A KICK WON'T STOP IT!

THERE COULD BE TROUBLE AHEAD!

LET'S HIDE IN THE TREE HOUSE!

SLAM!
WE'LL BE SAFE IN HERE.
LATER -
KNOCK! KNOCK! KNOCK!
WHO COULD THAT BE?
GULP! WE WEREN'T SAFE HERE AFTER ALL!

AHEM! THE SNOW MACHINE'S PRODUCED A LITTLE TOO MUCH!
DENNIS!
THE END.

SMIFFY IS IN BED AND LATE FOR SCHOOL. AGAIN. HELP OUR PEA-BRAINED PAL GET TO SCHOOL BY PLAYING THIS GAME. YOU WILL NEED COUNTERS AND A DUNCE SORRY, COUNTERS AND A DICE.
SNORE!
QUACK! QUACK!
!?!
THE ALARM CLOCK QUACKS. YOU CAN START.
2
3
CAN'T FIND YOUR WAY OUT OF BED. HAVE ANOTHER TURN.
5
6
SCRATCH!
OINK! GAASP!
PICK UP YOUR BAG FOR SCHOOL.
20
21
MISS A TURN BECAUSE YOU PICKED UP THE LAUNDRY INSTEAD OF YOUR SCHOOL BAG. OFFER TO DO THIS WEEK'S WASH AND YOU DON'T HAVE TO MISS A TURN.
TAKE THE WRONG TURN IN THE GARDEN. ON YOUR NEXT TURN, ROLL THE DICE FROM BEHIND YOUR BACK.
SMIFFY HEARS AN AMBULANCE AND THINKS IT'S AN ICE CREAM VAN. HAVE AN EXTRA SCOOP OF ICE CREAM AT TEA!
SCOOSH!
SPLUDGE!
WET CEMENT.
25
SMIFFY STOPS TO SING A SONG - WE DON'T KNOW WHY. SING 4 LINES OF YOUR FAVOURITE SONG THEN HAVE ANOTHER TURN.
27
SMIFFY THINKS 'WET CEMENT' IS AN INSTRUCTION NOT A WARNING. HOP AROUND THE ROOM AND MISS A TURN.
29
TOM PATERSON

18. Fred has suddenly forgotten about gravity. Throw again while he floats back down.
19.
20. Fred has stopped to ask an alien directions and he sends him back 3 spaces - how mean!
21.
22. Hitch a lift from a shooting star and move forward 4 spaces.
23.
24.
MAP
25. Fred is lost and has found an alien signpost. Miss a turn while he tries to work it out.
26.
27. A naughty alien has pinched Fred's shoes. You have to throw a 6 to get them back.
28.
29.
30. Fred has to jump over a meteor, move on 2 spaces.
31.
32.
33. The aliens challenge Fred to a thumb wrestle. Fred loses so go back 4 spaces.
34.
35. FINISH! Yippee! Yahoo! You've found Fred's bed and can go home. Wave cheerio to the aliens!
FINISH

Printed and Published in Great Britain by D.C. Thomson & Co., Ltd, 185 Fleet Street, London, EC4A 2HS. © D.C. Thomson & Co., Ltd, 2010.

CONTACT DETAILS By post: The Beano, D.C. Thomson & Co., Ltd, 2 Albert Square Dundee DD1 9 QJ
email: beano@dcthomson.co.uk phone: 01382 223131

PROMOTIONS promotions@dcthomson.co.uk
SYNDICATION syndication@dcthomson.co.uk
CIRCULATION circulation@dcthomson.co.uk
LICENSING start.licensing@btinternet.com

recycle
When you have finished with this magazine please recycle it.

For Advertising Please Contact:
Jack Daly 020 7400 1069
jdaly@dcthomson.co.uk
Sophie DeVault 0161 606 1350
sdevault@dcthomson.co.uk